Published 2007
Printed by Classical Conversations Multi-Media
in the United States of America

MW01485075

Words Aptly Spoken

Classical Conversations' Guide to

Classical Literature for Children

Volume A

Compiled and Edited by
Jennifer Greenholt

Classical Conversations Press, Seven Lakes, NC

Acknowledgments

Many thanks…

To the members of Classical Conversations, whose thoughts, input, and advice have gone into the creation of this book and whose support have made it possible;

To the many talented authors whose works I have been privileged to enjoy during the creation of this book.

Table of Contents

Title   **Page**

ii

Foreword

Learning to read is one of the most defining moments in life. It opens an unparalleled number of doors and possibilities, some of them life-changing. The books you read from that moment on have an enormous amount of power to shape your life. This is one of the characteristics that make quality children's literature so priceless.

Words Aptly Spoken: Children's Literature takes you into the world of award-winning children's and young adult authors. Many of the books in this collection have won the Newbery Medal, one of the most prestigious awards for American children's literature. But while these books were first and foremost written for the enjoyment and education of children, they are not only for children. The lessons they teach and the courage of the people whose stories they tell are ageless. Everyone can take something away from these books, whether it is a better understanding of responsibility and selflessness or a new appreciation for the ability to read.

As with previous collections, *Children's Literature* contains a series of questions about each work being studied. Review questions ensure that you understand the basic plot, characters, setting, and message of the book. Thought questions take the themes and ideas raised by each author and help you apply them to other, more familiar situations.

If you cannot answer some of the questions by the time you have finished the book, consider going back and reading over sections that you may only have skimmed the first time. One word of caution – do not merely "look up" the answers to the questions without reading the book as a whole. Later on, you will find that this habit makes it harder for you to read and understand more difficult books.

Children's Literature also introduces strategies for summarizing, creating chronologies and character charts, taking notes, and analyzing symbolism. Each of these skills will make reading and writing about classic literature a more fulfilling experience.

It is best if you have your own copy of each book so that you can feel free to highlight or make notes in the margins. If, however, you need to use a copy belonging to the library or to a friend, consider reading with a small notebook or pad of sticky notes nearby so that you can jot down ideas and connections while they are fresh in your head.

All this being said, take a deep breath and get ready to plunge into some great works of children's literature.

Reading Practice

This section is meant to give you a sampling of the skills which, at some point in your reading/writing career, you will need to use. It is not necessary to do all of these things with every book that you read. At the beginning of each book section, a particular skill is recommended for you to practice. If you would rather practice a different skill or work on several skills at once, feel free to do so.

Chapter summaries

After you finish reading each chapter, set the book aside and think back over what happened in that chapter. If necessary, re-read to refresh your memory. Then jot down the major events from the chapter. DO NOT write a chapter summary while looking at the book. If you need to look at the book in order to summarize what you have read, you should probably go back and read it again before you continue.

A chapter summary should be written in full sentences, and should be no longer than one paragraph (4-5 sentences). Essentially, a chapter summary is a way for you to look back and remember what you have read so far. Chapter summaries are also very helpful when you are finding quotes for a paper or studying for a test.

Notes

The first thing to remember is that note taking is not about abbreviating exactly what the book (or speaker) says. Instead, it is about picking the most important information and putting it into your own words. As with chapter summaries, it is important to take notes after you have finished reading. The best way to take notes is to read a paragraph or two at a time, set the book down, and jot a few notes (in your own words) to remind you of the main ideas. Keep in mind that notes do not have to be in full sentences. Unlike chapter summaries, notes are not just focused on the action of the story; they may also help you remember examples of symbolism, important quotes, recurring themes, or even hints about events to come.

Note-taking is very important in any academic setting. If you can learn to take good notes, you will have an easier time avoiding unintentional plagiarism. Plagiarism means taking someone else's words and using them as your own without giving credit to the author. Plagiarism is a serious offence in most colleges and universities. To avoid plagiarizing, make sure you include quotation marks ("-") if you use the author's exact words in your note, and be careful that your notes are not just a re-worded version of the original.

Character charts

The large majority of books you read will have at least three or four characters in addition to the protagonist (main character). Some books have so many characters that it is difficult to keep them all straight! One tool that will help you is a character chart. A character chart is simply a list of the people you encounter in the book, with a few brief notes or arrows indicating relationships between the characters. You can also write comments about the characters' personalities, looks, or actions. As you read, keep your character chart nearby. Then, if you have a question about how two characters are related, you will not have to search through the book to find the page where the characters were introduced. A character chart may also help you write essays, especially character sketches.

Chronologies

Some authors use flashbacks or have two sequences of action running at the same time. It can be helpful to see the events of a book or chapter as they occur in chronological order. You can do this by drawing out a timeline. You can break the timeline down into segments for each chapter or the more traditional days/hours, depending on the time span of the story. As you look at your timeline, draw "arrows of influence" between earlier and later events of the book.

As you prepare your timeline, think about whether some chapters have more events (actions) than others. Are the chapters with less action shorter? If not, what takes the place of action? You should be able to see patterns emerge; areas the author seemed to think were worth dwelling on. What important messages or themes are brought up in these sections of the plot? How are these messages played out later on? Do they factor into the conclusion of the story? Into the main characters' development? All of these considerations will help you when it comes time to write essays.

Layout maps

Fantasy novels are often set in a world that the author of the book has created. It can be helpful to draw a map of the fantasy world. You may want to do the same thing for some books set in the real world. Mark down place names, and any major events that happen at each location. Another option is to write down some of the important historical features of each location. If the characters travel around a lot, use colored pencils to mark out their journeys. For a good example of this, look at the maps accompanying J.R.R. Tolkien's *The Hobbit* or *The Lord of the Rings*. If the book is set in the real world, use an atlas to copy the basic shape of the country, and then draw in your own details.

Glossaries of terms

Some books use words with which you may not be familiar. These may be technical terms (in some science fiction books, for example), local slang (*Shiloh* is a good example of this), or made-up words (as in some fantasy novels). Some authors also use big or old-fashioned words that you may not recognize. If you come across an unfamiliar word, take a minute to write it down, along with a brief definition. That way if you see the word again, you can refer back to your glossary. This is also a great way to expand your vocabulary.

Going Deeper

As you will discover, one of the most exciting things about classic literature is that it has multiple levels of meaning. On the surface, the book may be enjoyable to read because it has good action and interesting characters. But if you read it again, you may begin to see parallels in the way different characters deal with their problems. A third reading may lead you to ponder similar struggles in your own life. Authors use a variety of tools to craft the layers of meaning in their books. This section will explore some of those methods and give you tools for reaching a deeper understanding of the books you read.

Recognizing parallel themes

Authors sometimes use sub-plots, minor events or problems within the larger situation, to reflect the conflict in the main plot. If, for example, the central conflict of the book revolves around a character's selfishness, then perhaps that character will have an argument with a sibling because he/she does not want to share. Other times, a minor, one-dimensional character serves as a mirror by which another character sees his or her flaws magnified.

Tracing character development

Books would not be nearly as interesting if the main characters remained unchanged. One of the characteristics of a classic work of literature is that the characters grow or change in some way. After you have read each book, go back and look at the characters' words and actions at the beginning and at the end of the book. Have their attitudes changed? Have their outlooks on life changed? Have they become more sensitive? Braver? Have they learned patience? Try to trace the events that have contributed to these changes.

Illustrating your mental images

One of the most difficult jobs for a filmmaker is to turn a well-known book into a movie. Why? Because so many people have mental images of the settings and characters in the book, and everyone has a different mental image.

When you read a book section that seems particularly "vivid", take a minute to sketch your image of the scene. Compare your drawings with another person who has read the same book. Try to figure out why the drawings are different. If possible, look at an illustrated copy of the book, and see how close your vision of the scene comes to that of the illustrator. Think about the emotive quality (ability to produce a particular emotion) of certain words. How did the author use these words to create a picture in your mind? How can you, in your own writing, use word choice to convey a certain mood?

Identifying symbolism

When is a tree not a tree? Trick question, right? Not necessarily. In literature, sometimes a simple object or action represents something much larger. This is often referred to as symbolism. For example, in the book *The Bronze Bow*, the sandals Daniel must wear when he returns to the village, and the cleansing rituals he must follow are symbolic of the captivity he feels when he is in the village.

Sometimes the symbol is not a specific thing, but rather a pattern of events that is repeated on a small and large scale. In *The Hiding Place*, Corrie ten Boom identifies symbolism in her own life. When Father does not let Corrie carry his briefcase because it is too heavy for her, she reflects that this is similar to the way in which God sometimes denies us full knowledge because he knows we are not strong enough to bear it.

As you read, be on the lookout for symbolism. Authors rarely put anything in "just because." Try to think about how small events and interactions reflect the larger lessons of the book. And even though the "dark and stormy night" with which the cartoon character Snoopy began his writing is a bit overdone, keep in mind that something as simple as a rainstorm or planting a tree may reflect a transition in the book or in the life of a character.

Exposing the "normal"

Have you ever stopped to consider why you would not wear a hat in church? Why "boys don't cry"? Why it's impolite to ask someone how much money they make? These and many other assumptions are part of our culture, part of the invisible rulebook that influences our behavioral choices. We act according to similar assumptions every day, often without being aware we are doing so.

A well-written book also presents you with a scenario in which certain things are taken for granted. If you read a book set in the Civil War, most likely the female characters will wear dresses and perhaps corsets. The characters will do this without questioning, and you, the reader, will be expected not to question it either. In many ways, this is the mark of a well-written book set outside the reader's place and time. The author needs you to accept the characters' world, with all its peculiarities, as a place as normal as your own world.

Sometimes it is easy to be swept up in the author's view of the universe, to blindly accept the philosophies, worldview, and actions of the characters without question. In most cases, this is harmless and one of the great joys of reading – being carried away by the author's imagination. But at the same time it is wise to be aware of the subtle messages the author is presenting.

When you read, ask yourself these questions: What is the author hoping you will accept as normal? What is he/she trying to convince you to believe? Do the consequences of the characters' actions (or lack thereof) encourage you to follow their example? In most cases, the messages you find will relate to the period in which the book is set, and may provide an interesting glimpse of history. But occasionally, the author's message may encourage you to disregard morals "under [fill-in-the-blank] circumstances" or to agree that "obviously [fill-in-the-blank] is true about the world." So when you read, enjoy the details that make living on Mars or in the 18th century seem equally possible, but try to avoid getting so swept away that you forget to think about what the author is really saying.

The Magician's Nephew

By C.S. Lewis

Introduction

Clive Staples Lewis (1898-1963) is one of the most prominent names in Christian literature. After a personal investigation of Christianity, Lewis went on to write books on topics ranging from pain and loss to the meaning of Biblical love. Lewis also wrote a number of Christian-themed children's and science fiction novels. *The Magician's Nephew* was published in 1955. It is the prequel to Lewis' famed *Chronicles of Narnia*, although it was written after most of the other books in the series. *The Magician's Nephew* introduces readers to the world of Narnia, and sets the stage for the next book, *The Lion, the Witch, and the Wardrobe*.

Reading Practice

Layout map

Going Deeper

Expose the "normal"

Chapter 1

Review Questions

1. How did Polly and Digory meet?
2. Why was Diggory unhappy?
3. Which house did Polly and Digory enter from the tunnel?
4. What was the humming noise that Polly heard?
5. What did Uncle Andrew want to give Polly?
6. What happened when Polly took the gift?

Thought Questions

1. How did Polly and Digory get to know one another?
2. Were they very similar? How were they different?
3. Think about one of your friends. How did you get to know each other?
4. Did you like the same things, or were you put in a situation where you needed each other?

Chapter 2

Review Questions

1. Who was Mrs. Lefay? What was unusual about her?
2. Where had Mrs. Lefay gotten her box?
3. What was in the box Mrs. Lefay gave Uncle Andrew?
4. What was the difference between the yellow and green rings?
5. Why didn't Uncle Andrew want to go to the Other Place?
6. How did Uncle Andrew convince Digory to take the ring?

Thought Questions

1. Uncle Andrew thought promises and rules only applied to little boys, servants, and women. What does this tell you about his views on children? Women? Servants?
2. Do you think someone should be free from moral rules if they are particularly smart or powerful?
3. Do superheroes obey the law? Are the results of their actions generally good or bad?
4. Do you think Uncle Andrew was a coward? Explain.
5. Before he left, Digory said "he could not decently have done anything else." Do you agree? Why?

Chapter 3

Review Questions

1. Where did Digory go when he put on the yellow ring?
2. How did Digory describe the wood?
3. Who did Digory meet beside the pool?
4. What prevented Polly and Digory from going straight home?
5. What did Digory almost forget to do (just before they set out to explore another world)?
6. Why didn't the yellow rings take Polly and Digory into another world?

Thought Questions

1. What kind of scientific tests do you think are ethical (using human volunteers, yourself, animals)?
2. How do you determine what is and is not ethical?
3. How had Uncle Andrew misunderstood the function of the rings?
4. Is it wise to use something you don't understand completely?

Chapter 4

Review Questions

1. Describe the new world Digory and Polly entered.

2. How did Polly and Digory know this new world was very old?
3. What did the children see in the great hall?
4. How did the faces change as the children went farther into the room?
5. Did Polly want to strike the bell? Why or why not?
6. What about Digory? Why?
7. What happened when the bell was struck?

Thought Questions

1. Digory described the last woman in the hall as both very beautiful and very cruel. Is this possible?
2. What does this tell you about beauty?
3. What do you think the poem on the pillar meant?
4. Would you have struck the bell? Why or why not?
5. Is curiosity a bad thing? When does it become a bad thing?

Chapter 5

Review Questions

1. How did the Queen, Polly, and Digory get through the doors?
2. Who destroyed Charn? How was it destroyed? Why was it destroyed?
3. How did Polly and Digory escape Charn? What went wrong with their escape?

Thought Questions

1. What did Digory think of the Queen? What did Polly think?
2. Why do you think the two children saw the Queen differently? Which one was right?
3. How were the Queen and Uncle Andrew similar? How were they different?

Chapter 6

Review Questions

1. What did the trip back to the Wood between the Worlds teach the children about the rings?
2. How did Jadis get to London?
3. What was Uncle Andrew's silliness?

Thought Questions

1. What did Polly want to do to Jadis in the Wood between the Worlds? Why? Do you agree with her?
2. What do you think is the mark of a magician?
3. If you did wicked things over and over again, would it change your appearance? If so, how?

Chapter 7
Review Questions

1. Why couldn't Polly go back to help Digory?
2. How did Digory plan to get rid of the Witch?
3. Why did Digory suddenly want to go back to the wood? What prevented him from going?

Thought Questions

1. Would it have been wrong for Digory to leave Jadis in London? Was she his responsibility?

Chapter 8

Review Questions

1. How many people did Digory bring with him to the wood? Who were they?
2. Which world did the group enter by mistake?
3. What happened when the voice began to sing?
4. Who was the singer?

Thought Questions

1. If the music and singing were so beautiful, why do you think the Witch hated them?
2. What is the most beautiful sound you have ever heard? How did it make you feel?
3. What do you imagine the Lion's singing sounded like?

Chapter 9

Review Questions

1. How did the trees appear?
2. What happened when the Witch threw the iron bar at the Lion?
3. What did Uncle Andrew want to do with the new world?
4. Why did Polly compare Uncle Andrew to the Witch?
5. What did the Lion do to the animals he selected?

Thought Questions

1. Polly thought everything that was made came "out of the Lion's head". Explain her logic.
2. What parallels can you find between this creation story and the one found in Genesis 1-2?
3. Were Uncle Andrew's plans for the new world wrong? Why or why not?
4. Is it a good thing to use the resources around you? When does it become a bad thing?

Chapter 10
Review Questions

1. What was the first joke?
2. Why couldn't Uncle Andrew hear Aslan talking?
3. Did Strawberry remember the Cabman?

Thought Questions

1. Have you ever convinced yourself that something wasn't true?
2. Is it hard for you to accept being wrong? What does it take to convince you?
3. How do your ideas about other people impact the way you see them?

Chapter 11

Review Questions

1. What did the animals think of Uncle Andrew? What did they do to him?
2. What did Aslan say when Digory asked him for help?
3. How did the Cabby's wife get to Narnia?
4. What did Aslan say were the qualities a king needed to have?
5. Who were the first king and queen of Narnia?

Thought Questions

1. How did the animals view humans? Was it different from the way you think about animals?
2. Is it ever a good thing to stereotype (make assumptions about) people based on the way they look?
3. Do you think it was fair for Aslan to blame Digory for the Witch's coming to Narnia?
4. In your mind, how is a king different from other people?

Chapter 12

Review Questions

1. What did Aslan ask Digory to do?
2. What was Strawberry's new name? How did he get it?
3. Why did Digory and Polly bury the ninth toffee?
4. What did Fledge and the children hear just as they were about to go to sleep?

Thought Questions

1. Why do you think Aslan had tears in his eyes when he talked about Digory's mother?
2. Why did Aslan say that only he and Digory knew how powerful grief could be?

3. Fledge said although Aslan knew what the children needed, he liked to be asked. Do you think the same thing is true of God? Why or why not?

Chapter 13

Review Questions

1. Why didn't Polly and Fledge go into the garden with Digory?
2. Why didn't Digory take one of the apples for himself?
3. Who did Digory meet in the garden?
4. How did the Witch change after she ate the apple?
5. How did the Witch try to convince Digory to steal one of the apples?
6. What mistake did the Witch make?

Thought Questions

1. Digory asked, "Who would want to climb a wall if he could get in by a gate?" Is it that simple?
2. Did Digory owe Aslan anything, as the Witch asked?

Chapter 14

Review Questions

1. What did Aslan do with the apple Digory brought?
2. What was inside the animals' cage?
3. What happened to the apple? What was its purpose? Its power?
4. What did Aslan say would happen to the Witch because she ate the apple?
5. What gift did Aslan give Digory?

Thought Questions

1. Aslan said, "Oh, Adam's sons, how cleverly you defend yourselves against all that might do you good!" Explain. Can you think of an example in your own life?
2. How was Aslan offering an apple to Digory different from Digory taking one?

Chapter 15

Review Questions

1. What was Aslan's warning? His command?
2. How long were the children and Uncle Andrew gone?
3. What effect, if any, did the apple have on Digory's mother?
4. What did Polly and Digory do with the rings and the apple core?
5. How was Digory's apple tree connected to the tree in Narnia?

Thought Questions

1. Why didn't the children need their rings when they were with Aslan?
2. What other story is tied to the ending of this story? How did Lewis prepare the connection?
3. What do you think ultimately caused Uncle Andrew to learn his lesson?

The Bronze Bow

By Elizabeth George Speare

Introduction

Elizabeth George Speare (1908-1994) first won widespread recognition for her historical fiction novel, *The Witch of Blackbird Pond*, about the Salem witch trials. *The Bronze Bow* was published in 1961, and won the Newbery Award in 1962. Set in first century A.D. Galilee, *The Bronze Bow* explores themes of vengeance, forgiveness, and the meaning of God's victory.

Reading Practice

Chapter summary

Going Deeper

Trace character development

Chapter 1

Review Questions

1. What marked Daniel as a Galilean?
2. For whom was Daniel waiting? Why?
3. What message did Daniel wish to send, and to whom?
4. What did Joel and Thacia do before they ate? Why did it surprise Daniel?
5. Why had Daniel joined the robbers?
6. Why didn't Joel want to move to Capernaum?
7. How did Daniel view the Roman presence?
8. Who was Rosh?

Thought Questions

1. If you were away from home for 5years, would you forget people, places, and memories?
2. What gives a slave or a bound person the right to run away?
3. Is freedom a natural right? Defend your answer.
4. Can you ever permanently quiet your conscience? How?
5. What is the difference between a Bandit and a Hero? Can a person be both?

Chapter 2

Review Questions

1. For what did Rosh need Daniel?
2. How did Daniel convince Joel to go? What did Joel do instead?
3. What was Daniel's role in the plan?
4. What happened to Joel when he tried to help?
5. How did Joel respond to Rosh's threats?
6. Who took charge of the slave?
7. What did Samson do once he was free?

Thought Questions

1. If you are enslaved, does it matter who your master is? Why or why not?
2. Why do you think it mattered to Rosh that the slave slept free?
3. Is it possible to get satisfaction from a life driven by violence? Explain.

Chapter 3

Review Questions

1. What made it difficult for Daniel to look after Samson?
2. Why did Daniel resent Samson?
3. Who came looking for Daniel? What news did he bring?
4. Why didn't Simon want to join Rosh?
5. Why did the two men need to bathe before reaching the village?
6. What was the matter with Daniel's sister?
7. What was the "pauper's share"?
8. Where did Daniel's grandmother work? What did she do?

Thought Questions

1. Is it possible to disagree with someone's methods if you have the same goal? Explain.
2. Is it ever shameful to be poor? If so, when?
3. Why did Daniel feel threatened by Leah?
4. Why do you think Daniel no longer felt at home in the village?

Chapter 4

Review Questions

1. Why did Simon want Daniel to go with him to the synagogue?
2. How did Daniel explain his sister's strange behavior?
3. What did Daniel hope Jesus would say?

4. Why had the people of Nazareth tried to kill Jesus?
5. What happened as Daniel was returning home?
6. In Daniel's eyes, how did Jesus and Rosh compare?

Thought Questions

1. Do you think Leah had a mental disorder? If so, what kind? Explain.
2. What is a Zealot? Do you think Jesus was a Zealot? Why or why not?
3. Answer Daniel's question – where does the call of Jesus lead?
4. Why did Daniel leave the village?

Chapter 5

Review Questions

1. Why did Daniel want to find Joel? What was Rosh's response?
2. Describe Capernaum.
3. Why did Daniel leave the place where Jesus was teaching?
4. How was Daniel welcomed at the house of Hezron?
5. What actions of the Hezron family did Daniel describe as "heathen"?
6. How did Daniel insult Rabbi Hezron?
7. What did Hezron say in response to Daniel's accusations?
8. What was Israel's "one great strength" according to Hezron?
9. What did Daniel lose?

Thought Questions

1. While Daniel was gone, had things change on the mountain? If not, why was he disillusioned?
2. Explain the quote, "He's got too much to lose."
3. Do you think the Jews had lost their pride because they were civil to the Roman soldiers?
4. Why do you think Malthace shrank back from Daniel?
5. Did Hezron and Daniel react angrily to Joel's suggestion for the same reason? Explain.
6. Did Daniel judge the Romans collectively or as individuals? Was that fair? Why or why not?
7. Was Rabbi Hezron right about Israel's "one great strength"? Discuss.

Chapter 6

Review Questions

1. What happened at the well?
2. Where did Daniel seek shelter?
3. What did Malthace tell Daniel to do?
4. How did Joel react when he found Daniel?
5. Where did Thace and Joel hide Daniel?

Thought Questions

1. Why did Thace rescue Daniel?
2. Do you think Hezron would have turned Daniel over to the Romans? Why or why not?

Chapter 7

Review Questions

1. What did Hezron believe about fighting? What did Joel believe? Daniel? Thace?
2. Why did Daniel hate the Romans?
3. What had Daniel vowed?
4. Why couldn't Thacia take Daniel and Joel's vow?
5. What was the new vow?
6. How did Thace explain the bronze bow?
7. Why did Daniel decide to leave?

Thought Questions

1. Do you think God uses outlaws? Do you think he was using Rosh? Why or why not?
2. What did Joel mean when he said, "It is the same thing…Victory and the kingdom"?
3. What made the new vow different from the one Daniel had originally taken?

Chapter 8

Review Questions

1. Which historical man became Daniel's hero?
2. How did Thacia and Leah threaten Daniel's plans?
3. What did Rosh want Daniel to fix?
4. Why were the man and woman taking their son to see Jesus?
5. Why did Jesus say hand-washing was unnecessary?
6. Why did Daniel question the relevance of Jesus' words to the crowd?
7. What did Simon want of Jesus?

Thought Questions

1. Why were so many people curious about Jesus?
2. Why didn't the man and woman need to look at their son to know he had been healed?
3. Why do you think Joel stopped short of condemning Jesus?

Chapter 9

Review Questions

1. What job did Rosh give Daniel?
2. Why did Daniel give one of the daggers back to the man?
3. What did Rosh say when he found out?
4. What did Rosh tell Daniel he needed to do? Why?

Thought Questions

1. Does Rosh sound like Robin Hood to you? How are they alike? Different?
2. Do you think Rosh's actions were justifiable? Why or why not?
3. Is wealth a right or a privilege? Did the old man deserve to have his gold taken?
4. Is kindness the same thing as weakness? Explain.

Chapter 10

Review Questions

1. What message did Simon send?
2. Why had the villagers not entered the house?
3. What psalm did Daniel recite to his grandmother?
4. What sign told Daniel that his sister was not totally in the grip of the demons?
5. What happened to the grandmother?

Thought Questions

1. Why was Daniel afraid to spend the night in his grandmother's house?
2. Why do you think Daniel's grandmother expected him to return?

Chapter 11

Review Questions

1. What did Simon offer Daniel?
2. What was the hardest part of the job for Daniel to accept?
3. How did Daniel get Leah to Simon's house?
4. What did Leah find to occupy her time while Daniel worked?
5. How did Daniel show his contempt for the soldier?
6. What did the soldier see? How did Daniel react?

Thought Questions

1. How did Simon differentiate between a villager and an outlaw? Do you agree with him?
2. Did it surprise you to learn that Leah was a skilled weaver? Why or why not?

3. Why do you think the incident with the soldier made Daniel long for the mountain?

Chapter 12

Review Questions

1. Why did Daniel speak to the village boy?
2. For what reason had the boy's friends attacked him?
3. How did Daniel help Nathan?
4. Who did Joel bring to the shop?
5. What was the password of Daniel's band?
6. Why did the group change its meeting place?

Thought Questions

1. Does it shock you to think of someone selling their daughter? What modern social practices would have shocked people in Daniel's time?
2. What is the purpose of a brand? Does it undermine the power of giving your word? Discuss.

Chapter 13

Review Questions

1. What did Leah do with the coin she received for her weaving?
2. Why did Daniel ask Joel to speak to the young weaver?
3. Why did Joel go to hear Jesus speak?
4. What did the boys find when they returned to the house?
5. What did Daniel notice after Thacia's visit?
6. What made Leah laugh?

Thought Questions

1. Do you think Jesus and Rosh had anything in common? Would they have worked together?
2. Why do you think Leah allowed Thacia to see her?
3. In your opinion, what factors brought about the changes in Leah?

Chapter 14

Review Questions

1. What did Leah ask Daniel to explain?
2. What did Leah say about the soldier? How did she know?
3. What did Daniel find on the mountain?
4. Why did Rosh resent Samson?

5. Why couldn't Daniel take Samson back to the village with him?

Thought Questions

1. Why did Daniel think marriage was foolish?
2. What makes someone a master? Do they need the consent of the person they are mastering?
3. Did Daniel belong in the village or on the mountain? Explain.

Chapter 15

Review Questions

1. Why did Daniel go to hear Jesus speak?
2. Why did the overseers object to Jesus?
3. What story did Leah like to hear? What puzzled Daniel about the story?
4. To what did Daniel attribute the changes in Leah?
5. What did Daniel make?

Thought Questions

1. Why did it seem foolish to Daniel that a Jew and Samaritan could get along?
2. Is there a person or group of people with whom you think you could never get along?
3. Have you ever asked, "How long must the world go on like this?" What would your answer be?

Chapter 16

Review Questions

1. What did Rosh want Joel to do?
2. How did Joel propose to get the information?
3. Why didn't Thacia want to see Jesus?
4. What happened with the soldiers?
5. What did Thacia say to make Leah laugh?
6. What broke up the noon meal?
7. What did Daniel give Thacia?
8. What had the doctors said about Leah?

Thought Questions

1. Do you think Jesus would have condemned Thacia's actions?
2. Are all lies equally bad? Think carefully before you answer.
3. Why did Thacia admire Daniel's actions? In your opinion, were they wise? Brave?
4. What makes the world worth living in?

Chapter 17

Review Questions

1. What had Rosh done? How did the legionaries know he was responsible?
2. What role did Joel undertake for Rosh?
3. Why did Daniel's band join active service?
4. Why was Daniel disappointed in his boys?
5. What did the boys find on the road?
6. How did the Romans respond to the theft?
7. What happened to make the townspeople lose patience with Rosh?
8. How did Rosh respond to Daniel's warning?

Thought Questions

1. Do you think Rosh's plan was worthy of Joel's efforts? What purpose did it serve?
2. How does looting become a part of life during wars? Is it ever justifiable?
3. Was Rosh giving his life for the people's freedom? Explain.
4. Do you think Rosh's evaluation of the townspeople was fair? Why or why not?

Chapter 18

Review Questions

1. Who came to find Daniel?
2. What was the news?
3. What did Rosh say they should do?
4. What did Daniel decide to do?
5. Who became the official leader of the band of boys?

Thought Questions

1. Why did Daniel begin to see Rosh differently? Did Rosh change, or did Daniel? Explain.
2. What do you think about collective responsibility versus individual responsibility?
3. In what situations are you in favor of collective responsibility? With what exceptions?

Chapter 19

Review Question

1. Where did the band set up for their attack?
2. Did Daniel expect to survive?
3. What did the Romans do that threw Daniel off guard?
4. What unlooked-for help came to Daniel and the other boys?
5. How did the battle end?

6. What happened to Samson?
7. What did the boys lose that night?

Thought Questions

1. What was the difference between the fight and the glorious battle Daniel longed for?
2. Is war ever truly glorious? Explain.
3. Was the fight worth it, in your opinion? Defend your position.
4. How might the fight have been avoided?
5. How would a captain in Daniel's position decide which man to lose? How would you decide?

Chapter 20

Review Questions

1. Describe a life that is lived by the sword.
2. Why did Joel come?
3. Why did Daniel no longer see Rosh as his leader?
4. How did Daniel convince Joel to continue his studies?
5. What message had Thacia sent Daniel?
6. Why had Thacia not been forced to accept an arranged marriage?
7. Who were Jesus' enemies?

Thought Questions

1. Why is it easier to deceive someone who is angry at you?
2. Is it important to do things of which you can be proud? Why or why not?
3. Why was Daniel angry to hear that Thacia refused to choose a husband?
4. Do you think people serving in the military should get married? Discuss.

Chapter 21

Review Questions

1. Why did the priests from Judea question Jesus?
2. Why did Daniel feel the need to speak to Jesus?
3. What, according to Jesus, was the enemy?
4. Why couldn't Daniel follow Jesus? What did Jesus ask him to give up?
5. How did Jesus respond when he heard about Daniel's vow?

Thought Questions

1. Can freedom ever come from vengeance and hate? Explain.
2. Can you repay love with hate?
3. Is that what Daniel was trying to do?

4. Do you think Daniel's was a vow of hate?
5. Do you treat vows as if they are sacred? Why or why not?

Chapter 22

Review Questions

1. What set Daniel apart from the other young men?
2. Why did Daniel leave the festival?
3. What was Leah's surprise at dinner?
4. Where had she gotten it?
5. How did Leah know the Roman?
6. What did Daniel make her promise?
7. Why did Daniel know he could not take vengeance on the Roman?
8. How had Leah changed when Daniel returned?

Thought Questions

1. What were Daniel's real motives for going to the festival?
2. What are some other ways of fighting?
3. Why do you think Leah was unafraid of the Roman?
4. Have you ever done something you later regretted but were unable to undo? Explain.

Chapter 23

Review Questions

1. What was Daniel's hope for Leah?
2. Where had Jesus gone when Daniel arrived in Capernaum?
3. Why did the people call Jesus "Messiah"?
4. What had Jesus offered Simon?
5. How did Simon know God had not forgotten Israel?
6. What did Daniel want in a leader?
7. What was left to Daniel?

Thought Questions

1. Why did encounters with Jesus remove guilt? Did they change facts?
2. What did they change?
3. What did Simon mean when he said he already had the kingdom?
4. Does faith always mean "to choose, not knowing"?
5. Why would someone make that choice?

Chapter 24

Review Questions

1. Why couldn't Daniel seek a new band of Zealots?
2. What happened to Leah after the goat died?
3. What did the prospect of Leah's death mean to Daniel?
4. Who came to inquire about Leah? How did Daniel respond?
5. Who arrived at Daniel's house that afternoon?
6. What did Daniel decide when he looked at Jesus? What did he realize?
7. What happened to Leah?
8. What new vow did Daniel and Thacia make?
9. What did Daniel do in response to Jesus' gift?

Thought Questions

1. Why did Daniel say, "They could not learn to hope again"?
2. Is it harder to trust after you have been betrayed? If so, why?
3. Does freedom need a purpose to accompany it? Why or why not?
4. Is vengeance better than nothing as repayment? Explain.
5. What did it cost Marcus to approach Daniel? How do you think he felt when Daniel refused him?
6. Why did Daniel feel free to love Thacia?
7. Did Daniel break his vow? Why or why not?

Number the Stars

By Lois Lowry

Introduction

Lois Lowry (1937-) spent her childhood traveling the world with her military family. Many of the experiences and relationships she formed during these travels have found their way into her books. Lowry has written more than 20 novels, winning the Newbery Medal twice. *Number the Stars* was written in 1989, and won the Newbery Award in 1990. In *Number the Stars*, Lowry looks at the events leading up to the Holocaust through the eyes of a young Danish girl.

Reading Practice

Character chart

Going Deeper

Recognize parallel themes

Chapter 1

Review Questions

1. Why didn't Ellen want to race Annemarie?
2. What stopped the girls' race?
3. Did Annemarie and Ellen tell their mothers what happened?
4. How did Mrs. Johansen explain the soldiers' unease?
5. What was *De Frie Danske*?
6. Who were the Resistance fighters? How did they operate?
7. What did Kirstie want to eat? Why couldn't she have it?

Thought Questions

1. Why wasn't Kirstie afraid of the soldiers?
2. Why did Mrs. Rosen advise Annemarie to be "one of the crowd"?
3. Is it usually better to stand out or to blend in? Explain.

Chapter 2

Review Questions

1. What kind of story did Kirstie want to hear?

2. Who was the ruler of Denmark? Where did he live?
3. Why did the people love him?
4. Why did it make Annemarie sad to think about Lise?
5. Why didn't the king of Denmark fight the Germans, according to Papa?
6. What was the one country the Germans did not occupy?
7. What had not changed for Annemarie?

Thought Questions

1. Why did the Danes love King Christian? Do you think he was a good ruler? Why or why not?
2. Would people today die for their leaders? If not, why not?
3. Do you think King Christian was right to surrender to the Germans? Explain.
4. Do fairytales ever change? If not, why not? If so, how?
5. Can you think of anything that doesn't change? Does that mean it is out-of-date? Explain.

Chapter 3

Review Questions

1. Why did Ellen's father dislike the wintertime?
2. What did the girls find at Mrs Hirsch's button shop?
3. What had Peter brought for Annemarie and Kirstie? For Mama and Papa?
4. What news did Peter bring?
5. How did Mama say the Hirsch family would earn a living?
6. Why did Annemarie think she would never be called on for courage?

Thought Questions

1. What does the swastika mean to you? What do you think it means to someone from Germany?
2. Did it harm the Germans to have Jews in business?
3. Why did they order the Jewish shops to close?
4. Annemarie said, "all of Denmark must be bodyguard for the Jews". Explain. Do you agree?
5. Do people die for each other in real life? Is there anyone you would die to protect?
6. Is anyone truly "ordinary"?
7. Have you ever been called on for courage? How did you feel about the experience?

Chapter 4

Review Questions

1. After what book did Annemarie and Ellen name their paper dolls?
2. Why did Kirstie throw a temper tantrum? How did Ellen get her to stop?

3. What were the Tivoli gardens?
4. Why was Ellen's New Year different from the Johansens'?
5. Why did Ellen come to stay with the Johansens?
6. Where did Papa propose to hide Ellen?

Thought Questions

1. Why did Kirstie remember the "fireworks"? Was Mama right to lie to her?
2. Do you think King Christian felt sad or proud after he blew up his own navy? Why?
3. When do you think children are old enough to be told about serious things?
4. What makes someone old enough to hear a difficult truth?
5. What did "relocation" really mean for the Jews?

Chapter 5

Review Questions

1. What did Ellen want to be when she grew up?
2. How did Lise die?
3. What awakened the girls? What did the soldiers want to know?
4. What did Ellen need to remove? Why?
5. Why didn't the soldier believe Ellen was Annemarie's sister? How did Papa fool the soldiers?

Thought Questions

1. Do you think of rain as happy or sad? Why does the weather influence our emotions?
2. Why did Ellen think it was worst to die young? Do you agree?
3. How did Papa know to get the pictures? Is it difficult to think quickly in an emergency?
4. How could Papa be so calm under pressure? Do you think he practiced lying? Explain.

Chapter 6

Review Questions

1. What had Papa hoped would happen?
2. Why did Mama say it was safer if she and the girls traveled alone?
3. Why was Papa's telephone conversation strange? What did it mean?
4. What did Kirstie tell the soldiers?

Thought Questions

1. Is education more important than safety? Does the answer change if you think long term?
2. Why did the soldier ask Mama abut the New Year? What was he hoping to find out?
3. Are dreams ever dangerous or harmful? If so, when?

Chapter 7

Review Questions

1. What was Uncle Henrik's boat called?
2. What did Mama warn Ellen and Annemarie?
3. Where was Ellen's necklace?
4. About what did Mama tease Uncle Henrik?

Thought Questions

1. What does it mean to look at something with "fresh eyes"? Can you think of an example?
2. If two girls had been in Sweden, looking at Denmark, what might their conversation have been like?

Chapter 8

Review Questions

1. What special treat did the girls have for breakfast?
2. What did the soldiers do with the farmers' butter?
3. To what did the code phrase, "weather for fishing" refer?
4. What sad event did Uncle Henrik mention? Why was Annemarie confused?

Thought Questions

1. Why are ghost stories told at night? What makes the dark frightening?
2. Were Mama and Uncle Henrik lying about Great-aunt Birte? If so, why?

Chapter 9

Review Questions

1. How did Uncle Henrik answer Annemarie's accusation?
2. Was Great-aunt Birte real?
3. Who came in with Peter?

Thought Questions

1. How brave are you? Does the question make you uncomfortable? Why or why not?
2. Is it possible to be brave and frightened at the same time?
3. Why did Uncle Henrik say it was better not to know everything? Do you agree?

Chapter 10

Review Questions

1. What happened in the middle of the night?
2. What did the soldiers ask Annemarie?
3. How did Mama explain the closed coffin?
4. How did Annemarie describe the world?

Thought Questions

1. Can true bonds of friendship be broken?
2. Is it possible to number the stars?
3. How does the Bible verse that Peter read relate to Annemarie and Ellen's situation?

Chapter 11

Review Questions

1. What was inside the coffin?
2. What did Mama give the baby?
3. What did Peter give the baby?
4. What did Peter hand to Mr. Rosen?
5. What caused the commotion at the doorstep?
6. Where was Uncle Henrik taking Ellen and the others?

Thought Questions

1. Why do you think Peter called Mama by her first name? What did it symbolize?
2. Annemarie described Peter's comment as, "Only a brief grasp at something that had gone." Explain.
3. What is pride? When is pride a good thing?
4. What are the sources of your pride?

Chapter 12

Review Questions

1. How long did Annemarie think Mama would be gone?
2. Why was Mama late?

Thought Questions

1. Is it harder to do something dangerous or to wait for someone else to do it? Why?
2. What makes waiting difficult?

Chapter 13

Review Questions

1. What happened to Mama?
2. What did Annemarie find at the base of the steps?
3. What did Mama ask Annemarie to do?

Thought Questions

1. Was it fair for Mama to ask Annemarie to do something so dangerous?
2. Would you have been willing to take the packet without knowing what was in it? Why or why not?

Chapter 14

Review Questions

1. What story did Annemarie think of as she ran through the woods?
2. Why had Uncle Henrik needed to guide the others?
3. What did Annemarie hear? What caused the noise?

Thought Questions

1. Do you ask questions when you read? When you watch movies? Why or why not?

Chapter 15

Review Questions

1. How did Annemarie act toward the soldiers?
2. What did the soldiers want to know?
3. Why did the dogs act strangely?
4. What was in the package?
5. Did Annemarie get to the boat on time?

Thought Questions

1. Were you surprised to see what was in the package?
2. Why do you think the handkerchief was so important?

Chapter 16

Review Questions

1. Why did Uncle Henrik agree to tell Annemarie about the Rosens?
2. What did Annemarie learn about Peter?
3. Why did the soldiers search the boats?
4. Why was the handkerchief so important?
5. Why did Uncle Henrik say the Rosens would be safe in Sweden?

Thought Questions

1. What does the word "brave" mean to you?
2. Have you ever become frightened after you did something dangerous? Why?
3. Do all wars end? Explain. Can you think of any counter-examples?

Chapter 17

Review Questions

1. How old was Annemarie when the war ended?
2. What happened to Peter?
3. Why weren't the Johansens able to bury Peter beside Lise?
4. What did Annemarie learn about Lise?
5. Where had Annemarie hidden Ellen's necklace?

Thought Questions

1. If Lise had told her parents what she was doing, do you think they would have let her continue?
2. Do you think young people should get involved in resistance movements? Why or why not?
3. Why do you think Annemarie wanted to wear Ellen's necklace?

Amos Fortune, Free Man

By Elizabeth Yates

Introduction

Elizabeth Yates (1905-2001) incorporated her Christian worldview into the historical novels and biographies that earned her recognition. *Amos Fortune, Free Man* was first published in 1950, and won the Newbery Award shortly afterward. It is based on the real life of an African prince who became a slave in America. In this book, Yates brings Amos Fortune to life, allowing readers to experience the meaning of life and freedom from his perspective.

Reading Practice

Chronology

Going Deeper

Identify symbolism

Africa 1725

Review Questions

1. On what occasion does the book open?
2. What was At-mun's role in the tribe?
3. Who was Ath-mun?
4. Who were the invaders?
5. Who did they kill?
6. Which of the At-mun-shi were left behind?
7. What did At-mun tell his sister?

Thought Questions

1. What do you associate with the word "pagan"? Does it have a positive or negative connotation?
2. Why didn't the At-mun-shi resist being captured?
3. What work was At-mun born to do? Could he realistically expect to do it in captivity?

The Middle Passage

Review Questions

1. What significance did At-mun's presence have for the At-mun-shi?

2. Why did At-mun keep his head up?
3. Why didn't At-mun attack during the night on the canoe?
4. Where was the *White Falcon* going?
5. Describe the ship's discipline.
6. How long did the Middle Passage take?
7. What was At-mun's "defect"?
8. Who became At-mun's master? What name did he give At-mun?

Thought Questions

1. Why did At-mun have to be especially brave?
2. What made the At-mun-shi "abashed and spiritless"?
3. Why do you think individual differences faded in the pits?
4. How did the pits transform men and women into animals?
5. What two things did At-mun want to remember? Why do you think he chose those two things?
6. Why couldn't the master of the *White Falcon* land his cargo on a Sunday?
7. Was this hypocritical? If so, who were the hypocrites?

Boston 1725-1740

Review Questions

1. What was Caleb's trade?
2. Who best understood Amos?
3. What changed after Amos and Roxanne's conversation about the Bible verse?
4. What is manumission?
5. Why didn't Amos want his freedom yet?
6. Who did Amos look for at the harbor?
7. What name did Amos plan to take when he was freed?
8. Why was Amos sold? To who was he sold?

Thought Questions

1. Is it ever kind to withhold freedom? Do you agree with Celia?
2. Is it necessary to learn how to use freedom? Explain.
3. "He will not give [his name] up until he can replace it with something of equal meaning." Explain.
4. In what circumstances and for what reasons would freedom be harder than slavery?

Woburn 1740-1779

Review Questions

1. How did Ichabod Richardson treat his slaves?
2. What request did Amos make of Mr. Richardson?

3. What did Amos give Mrs. Richardson?
4. How did that gift change Amos' purpose in life?
5. When did Amos gain his freedom?
6. Who did Amos want to marry?
7. How long did she live after they were married?
8. Why did Amos fall in love with Lydia?
9. How did Amos wage his war for freedom?

Thought Questions

1. How could slavery affect even something as natural as singing?
2. Do you agree with Amos' comparison of Sundays to white skin?
3. Do Christians today put emphasis on church attendance? Is it important? Why?
4. Why was it so important to Amos that Lily die free?
5. Why do you think slaves and former slaves chose to fight in the war?

Journey to Keene 1779

Review Questions

1. Who did Amos hope to marry?
2. For what did Amos ask God?
3. What did Amos take in exchange for his leather?
4. How long did Amos save to buy Violet and Celyndia?
5. How did Celyndia react to freedom?

Thought Questions

1. What is the "shadow" side of freedom?
2. Why didn't Amos complain about the unfair treatment he received from white people?
3. Amos said, "Some things are too wonderful even for a child, and freedom's one of them." Explain.
4. Have you ever experienced that kind of freedom?
5. Can you appreciate freedom as much as someone who has been enslaved? Explain.

The Arrival at Jaffrey

Review Questions

1. Why did Amos need to have extra money before moving?
2. Why was Violet nervous about the move?
3. Describe the village of Jaffrey.
4. What did the constable advise Amos and his family to do?
5. How did Parson Ainsworth greet Amos and his family?
6. From whom did Amos get land?

Thought Questions

1. Was Amos more of a king in Africa or America? Explain.
2. Why wasn't the constable free to welcome Amos?
3. How do you express thankfulness? Do you agree with Amos' way?

Hard Work Fills the Iron Kettle 1781-1789

Review Questions

1. How did Violet and Celyndia help Amos?
2. Explain the tanning process.
3. For what was Amos saving his money?
4. What does "Monadnock" mean?
5. Why didn't Violet like Lois Burdoo?
6. What did Violet do with the iron kettle? Why did she do it?

Thought Questions

1. Were Amos and his family better off in Jaffrey?
2. How does having a dream change a person? Is it possible to live happily without a dream?
3. Why were black people kept separate in the church?
4. An elder said, "What a pity [Amos] isn't white. He could do so much for the church." Does race affect your abilities? Discuss.

Amos on the Mountain

Review Questions

1. What did Amos decide to do with the money?
2. How did Amos and Violet decide who was right and who was wrong?
3. When did Amos become a landowner?

Thought Questions

1. Is there a difference between doing the right thing and doing something for the right reasons?
2. Which one do you think Violet did when she took Amos' money?
3. Does freedom have to be earned?

Auctioned for Freedom

Review Questions

1. In what new way did the people of Jaffrey come to trust Amos?

2. What was Celyndia's burden?
3. What is a "Vendue"?
4. Who did Amos buy?
5. What happened to Polly? Why was Amos grateful?

Thought Questions

1. Is it right that Amos had to earn his equality? Is equality a natural right? Should it be?
2. Why do you think the Burdoos were unable to improve themselves?
3. Why did Amos tell Violet about Africa?

Evergreen Years 1794-1801

Review Questions

1. Who became Amos' new apprentice? Why?
2. For whose sake had Amos done so many good things?
3. What did Amos want before he died?
4. What did Amos put in his will? What gift did he give the church? The school?
5. When did Amos die?
6. What did Parson Ainsworth write on Amos' tombstone?

Thought Questions

1. Why do you think Amos treasured Charlie's apprenticeship papers?
2. What did Amos mean when he said he would not "put himself in bondage again"?
3. Do you think people would stop causing suffering if they knew they were doing it?
4. How were Amos' gifts designed to free the white men? Do you think they succeeded?
5. What would you want your tombstone to say?
6. What do you think someone else would write about you?
7. After reading Amos' story, discuss what freedom means to you.

The Door in the Wall

By Marguerite de Angeli

Introduction

Marguerite de Angeli (1889-1987) first worked as an illustrator before she began writing books of her own. She wrote a number of children's books about lesser-known sectors of society, including immigrant children, Amish children, and racial prejudice against African-American children. *The Door in the Wall*, a story about a lame boy living in the Middle Ages, was published in 1949, and received the Newbery Medal in 1950.

Reading Practice

Glossary of terms

Going Deeper

Identify symbolism

Chapter 1

Review Questions

1. Who was Robin's father? What did his father's occupation mean for Robin?
2. What had happened after Robin's mother left?
3. How had Robin compensated for being unable to see out the window?
4. Why did Dame Ellen leave?
5. Who came to see Robin? Why did he come?
6. Where did the visitor propose to take Robin?
7. How did they travel?

Thought Questions

1. Do your parents' jobs place certain expectations on you? Why or why not?
2. Can you choose not to accept these obligations?
3. Is one of your five senses better developed than the others? If so, how did it become that way?
4. Brother Luke said, "Thou hast only to follow the wall far enough and there will be a door in it". Explain. Do you agree?

Chapter 2

Review Questions

1. Describe Brother Luke's cell.
2. What activity did Robin begin?
3. What did he make?
4. What happened in the corridor after Robin and Brother Luke left the scriptorium?

Thought Questions

1. Why were the rooms of monks and friars called cells? Discuss.
2. Where does your name come from?
3. Why do you think people were named for their occupation (i.e. John-the-Fletcher)?
4. Why aren't people named this way today?

Chapter 3

Review Questions

1. Where was Robin taken? Who showed him how to finish the cross?
2. Why did Robin become angry? How did Brother Matthew rebuke him?
3. What, according to Brother Luke, are the keys to healing?
4. What did Brother Luke say about Robin's letter to his father?

Thought Questions

1. Do you blame other people when you are angry?
2. Why do you think people need to blame someone?
3. Do you agree with Brother Luke that "a bright spirit helps [healing]"? Explain.
4. Is reading a door in the wall? If so, how?

Chapter 4

Review Questions

1. What was Robin's next project?
2. What happened at the brook?
3. How did Robin know he was well?
4. Where did Brother Luke take Robin to get the material for his crutches?

Thought Questions

1. Is it inspiring or discouraging for you to see others doing things you cannot do? Why?
2. Brother Luke said, "Crutches or crosses as thou'lt have it. ' Tis all the same thing." Explain.

Chapter 5

Review Questions

1. What message came to Robin?
2. How far away was Shropshire?
3. Who were Robin's traveling companions?
4. Why did the travelers get lost?

Thought Questions

1. What is a pilgrimage?
2. Was Robin's journey a pilgrimage? What did Brother Luke say? What do you think?

Chapter 6

Review Questions

1. Did the host at the sign of the Shepherd's Bush hold out hope for peace? Why or why not?
2. Why did Brother Luke mistrust the White Hart Inn? Were his fears proven right?
3. How did the travelers escape?

Thought Questions

1. Was Brother Luke talking about literal or figurative wrong turns?
2. Have you ever taken a wrong turning in life? How far away from the right road did you get?
3. How would the adventure have ended if Robin had said, "I'm lame; I can't do it"? Why didn't he?

Chapter 7

Review Questions

1. What was happening at Wychwood Bec.? Describe the event.
2. Where did the travelers spend the night?
3. Was Robin welcomed in Lindsay?
4. Who or what were the primary threats to Lindsay?

Thought Questions

1. Where do you think the idea for grand churches originated?
2. Is everyone capable of some service? Can you think of any exceptions?
3. Was Robin's workload excessive for a cripple? Defend your answer.

Chapter 8

Review Questions

1. Why did Brother Luke recommend swimming in cold water? (Give 3 reasons).
2. How did Robin win over Alan-at-Gate?
3. Why was the fog dangerous? What happened as a result of the fog?

Thought Questions

1. Explain: "It is better to have crooked legs than a crooked spirit." Do you agree?
2. How would you define success?
3. Have you ever met someone who seemed incapable of failure?
4. Does such a person exist?

Chapter 9

Review Questions

1. Describe the siege of the castle.
2. What was the final straw for the besieged people?
3. What did Robin propose to do?
4. Who stopped Robin on the way?
5. What was the signal for the attack?
6. Why were Sir Peter and Sir Hugh on bad terms?
7. How did John and Robin get into the town?

Thought Questions

1. How was warfare different in Robin's time than it is today? How was it the same?
2. What do you think was the hardest part of Robin's task? Why?

Chapter 10

Review Questions

1. Was the attack a success?
2. How were John and Robin rewarded?
3. Who arrived on Christmas Eve?
4. What did the king give Robin?
5. Where did Robin and his family plan to go after Christmas?

Thought Questions

1. How had Robin changed? Why would the changes make him fearful of seeing his parents again?

2. How did Robin's father react to the crutches?
3. Robin's father told Robin he "[could not] see whether or no your legs are misshapen." Explain.
4. What was Robin's door in the wall?

The Secret Garden

By Frances Hodgson Burnett

Introduction

Frances Burnett (1849-1924) moved from Britain to the United States at a young age. She initially started writing as a means of supporting her younger siblings. During her lifetime, she wrote a number of children's and adult novels, as well as several successful plays. *The Secret Garden* was written in 1909. It is set in England and explores the changing lives of three children who learn to appreciate life and beauty.

Reading Practice

Layout map

Going Deeper

Expose the "normal"

Chapter 1

Review Questions

1. Who was Mary Lennox? Why was she so bad tempered?
2. What was an "Ayah"?
3. Why did Mary stare at her mother?
4. Why was it so quiet when Mary awoke?

Thought Questions

1. Does being wanted affect a child's disposition? Explain.
2. Do people think only of themselves when they are sick? If so, why?

Chapter 2

Review Questions

1. Why didn't Mary miss her parents?
2. Where was Mary taken? Where was she to be sent?
3. Define "marred".
4. Why did Mrs. Medlock describe Misselthwaite as a queer place?

Thought Questions

1. How would you have turned out if you had grown up in Mary's situation?
2. Why do you think Mary was surprised to learn that Mr. Craven had been married?

Chapter 3

Review Questions

1. What was Yorkshire?
2. Describe the moor.

Thought Questions

1. Why didn't Mr. Craven want to see Mary?
2. In your opinion, why did he bring her to England?

Chapter 4

Review Questions

1. What awakened Mary in the morning?
2. Why did Martha like the moor?
3. What did Martha think Mary would look like?
4. Why was the garden locked?
5. Who did Mary meet in the gardens?
6. Why did the robin come, and to whom?
7. What did Ben tell Mary about herself?
8. Where did the robin live?

Thought Questions

1. Did Mary expect life in England to be the same as in India? Why? Did she like her life in India?
2. Can the color of your clothes affect your mood? The mood of those around you? Discuss.
3. What customs, if any, do you follow? Why do you follow them?
4. Does ignorance make you indifferent to the suffering of others?
5. Has anyone ever told you something unpleasant but true about yourself? How did you react?
6. Is it always best to bluntly honest?

Chapter 5

Review Questions

1. Why was it good for Mary to go outside?
2. Where did Mary go most often?
3. Why did Mr. Craven hate the garden?
4. What is "wutherin'"?
5. What did Mary hear? How did Martha explain the noise?

Thought Questions

1. What did you play with when you were younger? Why are some children content without toys?
2. Who do you think Mr. Craven blamed for his wife's death? Explain your answer.

Chapter 6

Review Questions

1. What did Martha suggest Mary do to amuse herself?
2. What did Mary decide to do instead?
3. Why didn't Mary ask permission to explore the manor?
4. Describe one of the rooms Mary entered.
5. Who did Mary meet behind the tapestry?

Thought Questions

1. Why do you think closed doors and locked places are so fascinating?
2. How did you learn to ask permission?
3. How can you tell when someone is lying to you?
4. Is it harder with some people than with others? Explain.

Chapter 7

Review Questions

1. Describe the moor after the storm.
2. What did Mary want to do? Why did Martha say she could not do it?
3. Did the robin remember Mary?
4. What did the robin show Mary?

Thought Questions

1. Do you think Mary was correct in saying no one liked her?

2. When you are cross at other people, how do you feel about yourself? Do you like yourself?

Chapter 8

Review Questions

1. What did Mary intend to do with the key?
2. What did Martha's mother say when Martha told her about Mary?
3. What did Martha give Mary?
4. How did Mary thank her?
5. What did Mary find?

Thought Questions

1. Was it stealing for Mary to keep the key? Why or why not?
2. Does it seem strange for Martha's family to pity Mary? Explain.
3. What do you think Mary meant by "Magic"?
4. How would you explain the things she called Magic?

Chapter 9

Review Questions

1. What made the secret garden so different?
2. Was the garden "quite dead"?
3. What did Mary do to improve the garden?
4. What did Mary want to buy? How did she get the things?
5. What did Mary ask Martha to explain?

Thought Questions

1. Is gardening natural? Explain.
2. Martha said, "Children's as good as 'rithmetic to set you findin' out things." Do you agree?
3. Why do you think Mary wanted to see Martha's mother and Dickon?

Chapter 10

Review Questions

1. How did the Secret Garden change Mary?
2. Did Ben Weatherstaff like Mary?
3. How did the robin "get at" Ben Weatherstaff?
4. Why did Mary ask Ben about the roses?
5. What did Dickon look like? How did Mary meet him?

6. How did Dickon know Mary was friends with the robin?

Thought Questions

1. Who was the young lady of whom Ben spoke?
2. What makes someone likeable? Is being likeable a skill or a gift?
3. Why do you think Mary told Dickon about the Secret Garden?

Chapter 11

Review Questions

1. Had Dickon known about the garden?
2. Were all the roses dead?
3. Why did Dickon think someone else had been in the garden?
4. How many people did Mary like?
5. What did Mary ask Dickon?

Thought Questions

1. What makes people contrary?
2. Do you think contrary people can be cured? If so, how?
3. How many people do you like? Have you ever thought to count? Why or why not?

Chapter 12

Review Questions

1. How did Mary describe Dickon?
2. Who wanted to see Mary? Why?
3. What did Mary ask for? How did Mr. Craven respond?
4. What had Dickon left for Mary?

Thought Questions

1. Do you think Mary was being deceptive when she asked for "a bit of earth"? Explain.
2. How do you think Mr. Craven felt about Mary? What makes you think so?

Chapter 13

Review Questions

1. What did Dickon's note mean?
2. Why couldn't Mary go back to the garden the next day? What did she do instead?
3. Who did Mary find?
4. Why didn't Mr. Craven want to see Colin?

5. How did Mary convince Colin not to demand to see the garden?
6. What did Colin show Mary?
7. How did Mary help Colin fall asleep?

Thought Questions

1. Why did Colin think he would not live to grow up? Did he really believe that?
2. Colin said he didn't want to live or die. What do you think he wanted?
3. Did Colin really hate his mother? Explain.

Chapter 14

Review Questions

1. How did Martha react when Mary told her about finding Colin?
2. What was wrong with Colin, according to Martha?
3. Of what did Colin remind Mary?
4. What was the "best thing [Mary] could have said" to Colin?
5. Who came into Colin's rooms?

Thought Questions

1. Why do you think Colin let Mary look at him? What made her different?
2. How important is it to have the will to live?
3. Explain Colin's comment, "I *want* to forget [being ill]."
4. Do you agree with Dr. Craven's advice?

Chapter 15

Review Questions

1. Why didn't Colin like strangers to see him?
2. What was the robin doing in the garden?
3. Had Dickon known about Colin?
4. Did Dickon tell his mother about the garden?
5. What did Dickon say would be good for Colin?

Thought Questions

1. Do people act differently when they are "housebuildin'" or first have a family? If so, how?
2. Explain, "You can lose a friend in springtime easier than any other season if you're too curious."
3. Was Dickon talking only about the robin when he said this?
4. Do you agree with Mrs. Sowerby that unwanted children almost never thrive? Defend your answer.

Chapter 16

Review Questions

1. How did Mary offend Colin?
2. What made Mary angry?
3. Was she being hypocritical?
4. Why did the nurse laugh?
5. What did Mr. Craven send Mary?
6. What ailed Colin, according to the nurse?
7. From what did his tantrums stem?

Thought Questions

1. Is it strange that Mary was excited about getting fatter?
2. What do you associate with the word "fat"?
3. How are our standards for health and beauty different today?

Chapter 17

Review Questions

1. What awakened Mary in the middle of the night?
2. What did the nurse ask Mary to do?
3. Did Colin have a lump on his back?
4. What did Colin agree to do?

Thought Questions

1. How might Colin have grown up differently if he had been around other children?
2. Is the truth always enough to convince people to put aside their superstitions?

Chapter 18

Review Questions

1. According to Mrs. Sowerby, what were the two worst things that could happen to a child?
2. What did Dickon say was good for sick people?
3. How did Mary make Colin laugh?
4. What did Mary decide to tell Colin?

Thought Questions

1. Do you think it is better for a child to be neglected or spoiled? Why?
2. What kind of damage does each treatment cause?
3. Why do you think Dickon seemed like an angel to Mary?

Chapter 19

Review Questions

1. Why did Dr. Craven come?
2. What, according to Mrs. Sowerby, do children learn from other children?
3. Why did Colin feel better when he woke up?
4. What did Dickon bring with him when he came to visit?

Thought Questions

1. Why did the animals make it easier for the children to converse?
2. Does meeting a new person make you feel awkward?
3. How do you start a conversation with someone you don't know?

Chapter 20

Review Questions

1. How did the children arrange to get Colin into the secret garden without being seen?
2. What orders did Colin give Mr. Roach?

Thought Questions

1. Why do you think the springtime and the garden had such a profound impact on Colin?

Chapter 21

Review Questions

1. How was Colin diverted from thinking about the old tree?
2. To what did Mary attribute the robin's arrival?
3. When did Dickon say Colin would walk again?
4. Who interrupted the stillness of the afternoon? Why was he angry?
5. What did the newcomer assume about Colin?
6. How did Colin prove him wrong?

Thought Questions

1. Do coincidences exist? Explain.
2. Did the garden belong to Ben Weatherstaff? Why do you think he was so protective of it?

Chapter 22

Review Questions

1. What was the Magic, according to Dickon?
2. How had Ben entered the garden? For what purpose?
3. What did Colin want to do before the sun set?

Thought Questions

1. How did Ben justify breaking orders and coming into the garden? Were his reasons valid?
2. Do you agree with Dickon's definition of Magic?
3. What causes that kind of Magic?

Chapter 23

Review Questions

1. What was Colin's chief peculiarity, according to Mary?
2. Which kind of flowers had Mrs. Craven especially liked?
3. What was Colin's scientific experiment?
4. Why did Colin want to keep his experiment a secret?

Thought Questions

1. Can you make nice things happen by saying they are going to happen? Why or why not?

Chapter 24

Review Questions

1. Who did Dickon tell about the secret garden?
2. Why did Colin have to complain from time to time?
3. What made it difficult for Colin to pretend to be ill?
4. How did Mrs. Sowerby help?
5. Where did Dickon learn about exercising?

Thought Questions

1. Was it fair for Colin and Mary to deceive the staff? Was it unkind?
2. Do you think someone really could grow fat on laughter? Explain.

Chapter 25

Review Questions

1. Why did the children avoid the robin's corner?
2. Why did the robin and his mate worry about Colin?
3. What did Mary and Colin do on rainy days?
4. What change did Mary notice in Colin's room?

Thought Questions

1. Why did Colin begin to leave the curtain open over his mother's picture?
2. Was Colin's father fond of him, in your opinion?
3. What does it mean to be fond of someone?
4. Are fondness and love the same thing? Explain.

Chapter 26

Review Questions

1. About what topic did Colin lecture?
2. How did Colin know he was well?
3. Who came into the garden?
4. What was Mrs. Sowerby's name for Magic?

Thought Questions

1. Is there a definite moment when someone becomes well, or is it a gradual process?
2. Was it appropriate for the children to sing the Doxology? What does "Doxology" mean?
3. Do you think God and Colin's "Magic" are the same thing? Explain.

Chapter 27

Review Questions

1. What made Mr. Craven feel suddenly alive?
2. What did Mr. Craven dream?
3. Who wrote to Mr. Craven? What did she ask him to do?
4. How did Colin meet his father? What was Mr. Craven's reaction?

Thought Questions

1. "To let a sad thought or a bad one get into your mind is as dangerous as letting a scarlet fever germ get into your body. If you let it stay there after it has got in you may never get over it as long as you live." Explain. Do you agree?

2. Can two opposite things exist in the same person or place (happiness and sadness for example)?
3. Was Mr. Craven a bad father?
4. How do you think Mr. Craven and Colin's relationship would be different in the future?

Carry On Mr. Bowditch

By Jean Lee Latham

Introduction

Jean Lee Latham (1902-1995) had a gift for bringing the historical to life. Her biographies of famous Americans, including Eli Whitney and Sam Houston, have been widely acclaimed. *Carry on Mr. Bowditch* was published in 1955, and won the Newbery Medal in 1956. *Carry on Mr. Bowditch* introduces the life of Nathanial Bowditch, a talented navigator, astronomer, and mathematician who was a true example of what it means to love learning.

Reading Practice

Glossary of terms

Going Deeper

Recognize parallel themes

Chapter 1

Review Questions

1. Why did Nat want to stay awake?
2. What bad luck had come to Nat's family?
3. How did Nat's good luck spell turn out?
4. What did Nat do with his food?
5. What did Granny ask Nat to fetch?
6. What prevented Nat from performing his good luck spell in Salem?

Thought Questions

1. Is there such a thing as bad luck? Discuss.
2. Would you go to your neighbors if you needed to borrow something? If not, why not?
3. Do you think it is boys' job to look after girls and women? Discuss.

Chapter 2

Review Questions

1. What is a privateer?
2. Why did Granny tell Father to take Nat with him?

3. What did Father say he would do if he had money?
4. Why did Father call himself a Jonah?
5. How did the sailor respond to Nat's offer?
6. Why did he tell Nat not to mention their bargain?

Thought Questions

1. Do you think privateers and pirates are the same? If not, how are they different?
2. Are ethics different during wartimes? Should they be? Give arguments for each side.
3. Why did Father ask Nat if it was better to go back to his trade? Do you think he knew the answer?

Chapter 3

Review Questions

1. What question did Nat answer in school? Was he wrong?
2. Why did Nat prefer arithmetic?
3. What did Father ask Master Watson to do?
4. Why did Master Watson think Nat was lying?
5. What news did Nat hear about the *Pilgrim*?
6. What had happened to Tom Perry?
7. What did a fisherman's people do when a fisherman died at sea?

Thought Questions

1. Do you prefer math or history? Why?
2. What makes math a precise subject? Are any other subjects equally precise?
3. How can you convince someone to believe you? Is it possible?
4. What makes books so valuable?
5. Why did people say those like Tom "died heroes"? What is a hero?
6. Does it do any good to say "things will get better"? Why do people say that?

Chapter 4

Review Questions

1. What kind of ship was the *Freedom*?
2. Why had Hab lied about being cold?
3. Why did the shipowners think the war was almost over?
4. What caused the commotion in the middle of the night?
5. Who was John Derby?
6. When was the peace announced?
7. What is "crowding sail"?
8. What does it mean to "lose your anchor to windward"?
9. Why did Nat have to leave school?

10. Why did Mother look at the stars?

Thought Questions

1. Why do people say boys shouldn't blubber?
2. How big of a difference does it make to give your side of the story first? Why?
3. How does inflation work? What are products really worth?
4. Why is paper money less stable than precious metals?
5. Are peace and absence of war the same thing? Why or why not?

Chapter 5

Review Questions

1. Who did Nat crash into? What did the man say to Mother?
2. What happened to Mother?
3. What happened to Granny?
4. What did Nat overhear? How did he interpret it?
5. Who were Ropes and Hodges?
6. What was Father actually proposing?

Thought Questions

1. Why did Nat and Mary say Father had "lost his last anchor to windward"?
2. Have you ever misinterpreted something you heard? How can you avoid doing that?
3. Why did Nat react so lightly to his indenture?
4. Was it right for him to mislead his family about his feelings?
5. Would anything have changed if he had told them how he really felt?

Chapter 6

Review Questions

1. Why wasn't Nat happy about Mr. Walsh's praise?
2. To what did Lizza compare being indentured?
3. What was the bargain between Nat and Mr. Hodges?
4. Why was there so much blank space in the Chancellery's catalogues?
5. How did Ben describe Nat?
6. What is "sailing by ash breeze"?
7. Why did Mr. Hodges give Nat a notebook?
8. How did the log work?
9. How was the log different from "keeping a log"?

Thought Questions

1. Does indenturing sound like a fair bargain? Why or why not?

2. Have you ever sailed by ash breeze? Explain.
3. What are some practical uses for math? Do you think about the fact that you are using math?

Chapter 7

Review Questions

1. What did Nat do in the evenings?
2. What did Mr. Ropes ask Nat to look up? How did Nat misunderstand him?
3. What does an almanac tell you?
4. What did the stranger offer Nat?
5. What prevented Nat from accepting his offer?

Thought Questions

1. Why do you think Nat put so much effort into his notebooks?
2. How do you learn best? How much time do you put into voluntary learning?
3. Do you think you would have the willpower to sail by ash breeze for 9 years?

Chapter 8

Review Questions

1. What caused the excitement in town?
2. Which book on astronomy did Dr. Bentley give Nat? Why couldn't he read it?
3. What tools did Dr. Bentley give Nat to assist him in learning Latin?
4. What did Nat overhear on one of his trips to town?
5. What did Mr. Ward tell Nat?
6. What did the news mean for Nat's dreams?

Thought Questions

1. What books did you use the first time you learned a language?
2. Do you think you could learn a language using Nat's method?
3. How do you respond to disappointment? Compare your way to Nat's way.
4. Is there an age limit on attending college today? Discuss. Why was there one in Nat's time?

Chapter 9

Review Questions

1. What had Mr. Hodges suggested to Mr. Ward?
2. What kind of math did Nat use to compliment Lizza?
3. Why didn't Mary want to marry David Martin?

4. How did Nat convince her?
5. Why, according to Elizabeth, did Nat read Latin?
6. What did Dr. Prince offer Nat?
7. From where had the books come?
8. What did Nat want to tell Lizza? What prevented him?
9. What did Elizabeth give Nat? Why?

Thought Questions

1. What are "summer doldrums"? Have you ever experienced them?
2. Does being happy take practice? How would you practice it?
3. What did Lizza mean when she said Elizabeth had "eyes in the back of her heart"?
4. How does a good mind help you deal with hardships? Does it?

Chapter 10

Review Questions

1. To what new field of study did Mr. Read introduce Nat?
2. Why did Mr. Jordy say Nat needed to learn proper pronunciation?
3. How did Elizabeth want to surprise her father?
4. Explain Elizabeth's analogy of the chair.
5. What happened to Captain Boardman?
6. How do you tell time by the stars?
7. What gift did Mr. Hodges give Nat in the note?

Thought Questions

1. Is pronunciation always important when you study a language? Defend your answer.
2. Do you think English pronunciation makes sense? Why or why not?
3. What is intuition? Did Elizabeth really know when her father's ship would arrive?
4. Why do you think the freedom following indenture caused such a shock for some people?

Chapter 11

Review Questions

1. Why were American ships being attacked?
2. Why was Nat indignant about the editorial?
3. Did Dr. Bentley agree with Ben? Explain.
4. Why did Captain Gibaut say America needed a navy?
5. What job did Captain Gibaut offer Nat?
6. What is a venture? What did Nat choose for his venture?
7. What changed Nat's plans?

Thought Questions

1. Dr. Bentley said, "We can't have freedom – unless we have freedom". Explain. Do you agree?
2. Can censorship ever be justified? If so, when?
3. Compare ventures to the stock market. Does one involve a greater risk?

Chapter 12

Review Questions

1. What two things did Mr. Derby forbid?
2. How were surveying and navigation different?
3. What did Nat propose to use to find their longitude? Why was Captain Prince skeptical?
4. How did the men respond to Nat's teaching?
5. Why did Nat teach them?
6. What do sailors call "getting around" something?
7. How did Nat explain his accuracy with the lunar?

Thought Questions

1. Why do you think Captain Prince became so gruff when it was time to sail?
2. Can book learning substitute for practical experience? Give examples for both answers.
3. Why would men choose to be sailors?
4. Can everyone learn?
5. Do you think knowledge would make sailors more or less likely to rebel? Explain.

Chapter 13

Review Questions

1. Why had Bourbon changed? What was its new name?
2. What had happened to the harbor? How did this change the *Astrea*'s plans?
3. What advice did Captain Blanchard give?
4. How had the Frenchmen tricked Captain Blanchard?
5. What did Nat find while studying?
6. What did Dr. Bentley tell Nat when he returned to Salem?

Thought Questions

1. Why did the leaders of the French Revolution insist on calling everyone "Citizen"?
2. Why did Captain Blanchard's tactic fail? Why did the Frenchmen want to take advantage of him?
3. Is anyone above making mistakes? Have you ever assumed someone was? What happened?
4. How important is one small mistake? Was Nat overreacting?

Chapter 14

Review Questions

1. What did Mary want to tell Nat?
2. Where did Mr. Derby want to send Nat and Captain Prince next?
3. Why was Mr. Collins upset with Nat?
4. What did Elizabeth do right before Nat left?
5. What was the legend of Machico?

Thought Questions

1. Would you prefer to be very happy and then become very miserable, or to remain neutral? Why?
2. Why did Nat think of Elizabeth as a child?
3. Why do you think Nat chose Lem Harvey for his watch?
4. Do you think Lem's training methods were effective? Why or why not?

Chapter 15

Review Questions

1. What was Lem Harvey's problem?
2. What did Nat offer the crew? What was their response?
3. Why was the weather "upside down" at the Cape?
4. What kind of ship approached the *Astrea*?
5. What, according to Nat, prevented Lem from learning?
6. What made the men think the sea was on fire?
7. Why did the other ship pass the *Astrea*?

Thought Questions

1. Nat said, "It did things to a man…to find out he had a brain." Explain. Do you agree?
2. Did Nat lie for Lem? If so, why?
3. How did learning change Lem's attitude? Why?

Chapter 16

Review Questions

1. What did Nat think about Sunda Strait? What did he recommend for the return voyage?
2. Describe the outrigger canoe.
3. What happened on the return trip?
4. Why wasn't it a matter of pride to have a ledge named for you?
5. Who was waiting for Nat when he reached the wharf? Why wasn't he excited?

Thought Questions

1. Why did Captain Prince roar when Nat talked about the Manila Harbor?
2. How did Nat's feelings for Elizabeth change during this voyage?
3. Which do you think would be worse – a leak or a fight? Why?
4. Does the age gap between Nat and Elizabeth seem significant to you? Why or why not?

Chapter 17

Review Questions

1. How did Mr. Blunt respond to Nat's criticisms?
2. What is a "signature" in publishing terms?
3. Why did David want Nat to be at the husking party?
4. What did a red ear of corn mean?
5. What did Nat and Elizabeth decide to do?
6. Why did Nat's attempts to reassure Elizabeth backfire?
7. What news did the Harveys bring?
8. Why did Nat prefer the French to the English farewell?

Thought Questions

1. Why do you think Nat wanted to officially join the Philosophical Library?
2. Was Nat an astronomer? What is a scientific label really worth?
3. Do women know more about love than men do? If so, why? Discuss.
4. Is "not worrying" more important than hearing the truth? Which would you prefer? Why?

Chapter 18

Review Questions

1. Why did Nat say he was going to check all the published figures and tables?
2. How did the Englishman tell Captain Prince to detect French spies?
3. Why did the health officer throw the logbook overboard?
4. Who did Charlie suspect of being a spy?
5. What did the gunfire mean?
6. What happened when the three French ships approached?
7. Why didn't Nat realize the danger was over?
8. What news did Captain Gorman bring?

Thought Questions

1. How did Nat help Charlie? Does busyness cure homesickness? If so, how?
2. Would you describe Nat as a "great scholar"? Explain.

3. Was it bravado or compassion that led Captain Prince to leave the convoy, in your opinion?
4. Do you agree with Captain Prince's advice about being completely honest with your spouse?
5. Does work help you deal with loss? Why? Is it a permanent cure, or just a temporary one?

Chapter 19

Review Questions

1. How had Elizabeth died?
2. Why was Polly being so good to Nat?
3. What was Elias Derby's last dream?
4. What honor did Nat receive?
5. What did Mr. Blunt ask Nat to do?
6. Why did Nat agree?
7. Did Nat and Polly say goodbye? If so, how?
8. What had happened to the *Astrea*'s first crew?
9. How did Captain Prince keep the new crew from deserting?

Thought Questions

1. What is consumption called today? Is there a cure for it?
2. What does it mean to say someone can "see around corners"? Do you know anyone can do that?
3. Why did Polly leave a note?
4. Are short or long goodbyes harder? Discuss.

Chapter 20

Review Questions

1. What did Lupe want from Nat? What did he offer in return?
2. How much math did Lupe know?
3. How many errors did Nat find in Moore?
4. What did this work inspire him to do?
5. Why was the trip to Batavia a failure? What did they do instead?
6. What made the alternate destination so complicated?
7. Of what did the Harveys accuse Nat?
8. Why had the *Betsy* wrecked?
9. What had happened to Nat's brothers?

Thought Questions

1. Why did Nat say, "Lupe was the worst of the crew, because he smiled"? Does that make sense?
2. Why did Mr. Towson have to learn to take lunars?
3. Is it better to use an advanced method that, if flawed, is more dangerous, but if accurate, is more reliable than the old way? Defend your position.

Chapter 21

Review Questions

1. What was Polly's explanation for Nat needing to write his book?
2. How did Nat fall in love with Polly?
3. Who decided to end the honeymoon early?
4. What did Captain Ingersoll and Captain Prince propose?
5. What did Nat do with his book before publishing it?
6. What happened to the *John*?

Thought Questions

1. Was the sea at fault for all the sailors' deaths? Why did Lois blame the sea?
2. Would other countries be more likely to pay attention to an American book today? If so, why?
3. Why do you think Polly cared so much about Nat's book?

Chapter 22

Review Questions

1. What analogy did Dr. Holyoke make about book sailing?
2. Where was Nat's book first published?
3. What was Nat's role on the *Putnam*?
4. What award did Nat receive from Harvard?
5. Who surprised Nat and Polly? What had happened to him?
6. Why did Nat keep changing the subject?

Thought Questions

1. Why do you think prophets do not receive honor in their own countries? Is this always the case?
2. Would you describe Nat as a prophet? Why or why not?
3. Why did Nat want to go to Commencement Day at Harvard?
4. Why was that day the proudest of Nat's life? Why did it mean so much to him?

Chapter 23

Review Questions

1. Why couldn't Lem sail with the *Putnam*?
2. What kind of storm did the *Putnam* encounter?
3. Where did the *Putnam* find pepper? What difficulties did they run into?
4. Why wouldn't Nat let more than two Malays onto the ship at one time?
5. Why was the trip home so difficult?

Thought Questions

1. Did Nat have any more duties on the *Putnam* on this voyage? Why was he more worried?
2. What did Nat come to understand about Captain Prince as a result?
3. What do you think makes fog so frightening?

Chapter 24

Review Questions

1. How did Nat know Chad's wake was straight?
2. What did Nat want to see?
3. How did Nat calm Corey?
4. Why, according to Lem, should Polly hope Nat did not come?
5. How long had Nat gone without shooting the sun?

Thought Questions

1. Which is more efficient in a fog, mathematics or traditional navigation? Explain.
2. Did Polly trust Nat or the math he used? Explain.
3. Did Nat ever not sail by ash breeze? If so, when?
4. Was Nat ever becalmed? If not, why not? What can you learn from his example?

Afterword

Congratulations! You have now worked your way through seven classic works of children's literature. Along the way, you have assembled a variety of reading and thinking tools that will be important in your future reading and writing experiences.

Beginning in high school and continuing through college, essays about literature are assigned with increasing frequency. Almost every author surveyed on the subject says the key to good writing is lots and lots of reading. Good reading can start in no better place than with the classics of children's literature. If you can read these books confidently, remember key points, pick out symbolism, and compare major events and characters, you will be well on your way to writing excellent essays.

Even beyond formal education, the ability to understand and discuss the ideas in great literature is an invaluable social skill. But there is more to reading literature than being able to carry on a conversation about the characters in your favorite book.

In today's society, the media has an enormous impact on the way people view the world. In your daily life, a million and one ideas will compete for your attention. Most of the messages portrayed in the media will encourage you to accept without questioning.

If nothing else, it is my hope that this book will give you practice reading (and, by default, listening and watching) with your brain on and fully functional. If you can do this, you will be better prepared to distinguish between that which is merely enjoyable and that which is worthy of applying to your own life.